P.O

PURPOSE OVER POINTLESS EXCUSES!

TOPICS
BULLYING
DEPRESSION
INSECURITY
LEADERSHIP
POTENTIAL
REJECTION
RESPECT
SELF-WORTH
WORTHLESSNESS

HOW TO DISCOVER THE POWER TO OVERCOME...
THE DEMONT POPE STORY PT. 1

BY DEMONT POPE

Purpose Over Pointless Excuses

Copyright © 2021 by Demont Pope & Associates, LLC

All rights reserved. No part of this book may be reproduced, duplicated, distributed, used or transmitted in any form or by any means including photocopying, recording, or other electronic or mechanical methods, without written permission of the copyright owner except in the case of brief quotations embodied in critical reviews and certain other non commercial uses permitted by copyright law.

ISBN: 979-8-9852363-1-6

Cover Design by: Crea8tive Geeks, LLC

Edited By: Niki Pope

Purpose Over Pointless Excuses

TABLE OF CONTENTS

INTRODUCTION..5

Chapter 1: HOW IT STARTED..................................8

Chapter 2: NINE DIFFERENT SCHOOLS................23

Chapter 3: ROUGH TRANSITION...........................37

Chapter 4: IDENTITY CRISIS..................................60

Chapter 5: MINDSET SHIFT....................................74

Chapter 6: CONSISTENCY......................................91

Chapter 7: FIVE STEPS..102

Chapter 8: ~~PERMISSION~~ PURPOSE GRANTED........120

ACKNOWLEDGEMENTS:

The first person I want to acknowledge is you. Whether you purchased or received this book as a gift, I am truly Grateful and I sincerely THANK YOU!

Next, I would like to acknowledge every Educator, Counselor, Pastor, Speaker and Mentor that played a role in my development over the years. THANK YOU!

I must also acknowledge my family and friends who challenged and supported me during this process. I dedicate this book to the memory of my twin sister Debrina and my uncles Anthony and Timothy Pope.

To my beautiful and loving wife Niki and five amazing kids, I am grateful for your love, patience and support. THANK YOU for sharing me with the world!

INTRODUCTION

My name is Demont Pope and my mission is simple; I am here to expose the truth for you today. Now me personally, I don't like being lied to. How about you? I know that question might catch some people off guard, but not you, because you get me, you agree. You don't like being lied to either. You understand me and I need you to know that I understand you too. That's why, when I'm done, you will no longer fall for the lie.

You will stand firm believing in yourself because you will know that YOU ARE THE TRUTH.

No, you are not a mistake. You are not an accident. You are powerful. You have something inside of you that's far greater than what's going on around you. You have a purpose for existing.

I am writing this book to share my story in hopes that you won't succumb to life's pressure. You won't fall for the lies that circumstances want you to believe and quickly unlearn all the negativity fed to you throughout your life. One thing

Purpose Over Pointless Excuses

I need you to remember is that there is always another side to every story. The problem with most people is that they get stuck on one side.

When you are constantly surrounded by negative circumstances and people, it can influence your entire perspective of life. It may strengthen some people, but for others, it can lead them to thinking that there is nothing better in this life for them.

This type of thinking is what I call a dream killer. It robs you of your inspiration and motivation. It causes you to get stuck on one side of a story such as poverty, struggle, drugs, gangs, violence, lack and sickness.

I need you to hear me when I say that abandonment, rejection, depression, and insecurity is not your identity. Although it is something you may be experiencing, it is not the end of your story. In fact, it's only one side of your story.

In this book, I will share some of my life's struggles with you and how I made it through. I will prove to you that you can change the narrative of your story and that you too can find yourself on the other side. My desire is that by the time you finish reading this book, you will be equipped with tools needed to help you identify and place your "Purpose Over Pointless Excuses"

CHAPTER 1

HOW IT STARTED ....

Purpose Over　　　　　Pointless Excuses

I was born in Atlanta, Georgia in March of 1984, just a few minutes before my twin sister, Debrina. People say it's pretty cool to have a twin and I believe that to be true. However, I'll never know for sure because, although I led the way into this world, Debrina would soon become a leader in her own right, as she preceded me out of this world; leaving me here to experience life without her. I was then considered what people call a "Twin-less Twin".

I am the youngest out of my siblings. My sister (Shan), my brother (Chris) and I share the same mother, Deborah. However, Chris and I also have two older brothers (Melvin Jr and Maurice) and two older sisters (Lisa and Mignon) from our father.

Yet, I still sit and imagine what life would be like if Debrina were still alive. Would we be close? How would she look as an adult? Would she act like me? Would I be overprotective of her? Would life not have been such a struggle if she were here?

March 25th is our birthday and it's both bitter and sweet for me. I close my eyes and imagine us shouting happy birthday to each other and hugging, with giant smiles on both our faces. That picture in my mind always seems to give me a warm feeling inside. The problem is that when I open my eyes, she isn't there.

You may be thinking to yourself, "Wow, that is tough" or perhaps you can personally relate to losing someone close to you. Either way, you are correct. No child should have to start their childhood this way, but the harsh reality is that no one gets to decide how they will be born or what their childhood will be like. They don't get to decide who their parents will be, their family or where they live. We are born with no knowledge of this world, which makes it that much easier to believe the lies.

Now let's talk about it.

As early as I can remember, my life was filled with violence and hostility. My father was a Vietnam Veteran who I looked up to. He was a man's man and what some considered a country boy, who would hunt and fish as often as possible. When I think back, I can see my father skinning fish, rabbit and deer in our family kitchen.

I have been told that the man who came back from Vietnam was not the same person that left because after the military, my father returned as a heavy drinker with a bad temper. It seemed like the alcohol made my father, not only verbally abusive, but physically abusive too. The older I got, the more aggressive my father became and would often get upset and lose control of himself. If you were present once my father reached a certain level of "drunk," you became a victim. He was verbally and physically abusive to my siblings and I, but regrettably, most of the time, the receiver of his abuse was my mother.

The first time I was suddenly awakened from my sleep by the sounds of yelling and screaming, followed by cursing and name calling is forever etched in my mind. I can still hear the loud smacks and thuds of my fathers hands connecting with my mothers body to this day.

One day, walking home from elementary school, my brother, Chris and I found our mother sitting on the front porch with a torn shirt and bodily bruises. Though she did not say much, there was something in the way she looked at us that that day. That look was indescribable to my young mind then, but now I know, *personally*, that it was the look of "enough."

    I am not sure who called them, but what I do remember is that four or five police cars, with two officers per vehicle, pulled up in front of our home. I mentioned before, once intoxicated, my dad did not discriminate on who he attacked, so, of course, he went toe to toe with multiple officers immediately. He yelled, kicked, and fought the officers until they were able to subdue him. I watched them pull my dad's arms behind his back and tie his legs together using zip ties in a technique I later found out was called hogtying.

    My dad was dragged down the driveway, picked up and, not so gently, thrown into the back of one of the police cars; head first.

    As suddenly as they arrived, they were gone. Not one single cop said anything to me nor acknowledged my presence whatsoever. Was I not worthy of acknowledgement?

    I can still see my dad in the backseat of the police car kicking at the window as they drove away.

Purpose Over Pointless Excuses

Watching the altercation that day between my dad and the police left me with such feelings of uncertainty. I honestly didn't know how to feel. On one hand, I was afraid *of* my dad and wanted my mom, my siblings and I to be safe. While on the other hand, this was my dad, so I was also afraid *for* him and wanted him safe too.

I don't remember how long I stood in that driveway, what I was waiting for or what to do next. All I knew was that he was gone.

My dad ended up going to prison for about a year for domestic violence and hasn't been active in my life ever since. As a matter of fact, one of the last things he said to me was that "even though you and Debrina weren't mine, I still loved y'all like y'all were." Wait! What?!

Is this who I am now? Is this my identity; a Twin-less Twin, a Fatherless Twin, or the young black boy who doesn't even know who his biological father is? Is grief, rejection and abandonment a part of my Purpose now?

Without my dad, my mom had to take care of us on her own. She did her best to create a normal environment;

walking my brother and I to and from school daily. Even baking cookies for us on the weekends.

Unfortunately, on the way to get me from school one day, my mother had an accident. She slipped and fell, breaking her ankle in 5 places. The doctors inserted a metal rod into her ankle to help her walk, but later found a bone pressing against her spine causing ongoing pain and an inability to work.

As an abuse survivor, my mom looked forward to starting her life over, only to suffer an accident that would prevent her from ever working a regular job. She did not let that stop her, as she immediately applied for government financial assistance to care for us. It was never enough though and to top it off, I secretly blamed myself for her injury. If she hadn't walked to school to get me, she wouldn't have fallen, and our lives would have been different.

These thoughts were irrational, I know, but my life was full of negativity. It was only right that I adopted a negative mindset and fell for the lies too, right?

I thought that once on government assistance our lives would get better. It actually went from just in-home violence to instability, lack and more struggles.

From the time my father left and we were approved for government assistance, relocating became my new way of life.

I can remember going to quite a few different elementary schools. Let's see; there was East Lake Elementary, Fred A. Toomer Elementary, Terry Mill Elementary, Peterson Elementary, Venetian Hills Elementary, and I finally graduated from William M. Boyd Elementary School.

We moved from the east side of Atlanta, GA to East Point, GA and finally ended up on the west side of Atlanta, all while I was still in Elementary school. It was very difficult for me, going to so many different schools because I had a hard time making friends. When I finally did make a friend, I ended up losing that friend because I had to move away.

Research says that during a child's early school years they need stability, adult interaction and opportunities to share their feelings with friends. Moving as much as we had to didn't afford me those opportunities, so I became insecure, passive and timid. I had no real sense of identity. I wanted to fit in with anyone because I felt like I had no one.

Also, as a result of attending so many different elementary schools, I still struggle trying to remember my teachers' names from any of them.

Relocating as often as we did, I discovered, firsthand, how mean and cruel peers can be to each other. It was never cool being the new kid all the time. All of the other students knew each other pretty well because they had been living in the same neighborhoods or going to the same school together for years.

But, nobody knew me. Though I didn't know them either, I really wanted to. I really did want to be accepted by them and have the type of friendship they had with one another. The harsh reality is, my peers did not feel the same way about getting to know me or becoming friends the way I did them.

In the fifth grade, we moved to the west side of Atlanta where we stayed for about three years. During that time, the west side was probably considered the roughest side of Atlanta and I was going to school with rougher kids.

I remember getting into a fight in the fifth grade with one person and it seemed like the entire class teamed up against me; the new kid. Awful.

I later discovered that what made those kids so tough was the poverty and the struggle in the environment where they were growing up. It seemed like they had to fight for EVERYTHING and they did not welcome outsiders easily.

Luckily, I survived that fight, but I also learned a valuable lesson that day. Guess what? I couldn't fight! That's right. I realized that I did not know how to defend myself.

Embarrassing right?

Tell me about it.

Being the new kid to the school and community, fighting was not my focus; being accepted was. So now I am the Twin-less, fatherless, rejected, abandoned, new kid on *every* block that can't even fight!

I know now that there was poverty in all the other communities we lived in over the years, it just seemed to be much worse on the west side of Atlanta to me during the time we were there. There was so much drug infestation, alcoholism, violence, poverty, and hopelessness everywhere I turned. Most people in the community where I lived had very few options. They could become alcoholics, drug dealers, drug addicts, or local gang members. Those are some poor options, I know, but I still just wanted to fit in and belong.

Discovery Moment

When things happen in life that are out of our control such as parents separating or constantly relocating, it can make us feel helpless. The adversity and challenges of how your life starts can either be used as *Excuses* that keep you from realizing your true potential everyday or *Motivation* to make necessary changes. When you're young, people like to tell you that you have plenty of time, but in truth, that's a lie. Most people wish they could change something about how their life started out. Unfortunately, we can't change the past, but we can change the direction of our future.

1. Imagine that you could change some things about your past, what would you change first?
2. Why?
3. What did you learn about yourself from that experience?
4. What are you willing to change in your life starting now that will make your life better later?

Purpose Over Pointless Excuses

PURPOSE NOTES

PURPOSE NOTES

PURPOSE NOTES

CHAPTER 2

9 DIFFERENT SCHOOLS...

After graduating from Boyd Elementary school, next up was Middle School. My family was still living on the west side of Atlanta at this time on a street called Gun Club Road. No seriously. I actually lived in a poverty stricken neighborhood, full of violence, on a street named GUN CLUB! Well, Gun Club intersected with a main street called Hollywood Road. Now although the street was called Hollywood, it was far from the one that you hear about in the movie world. I can promise you that!

Every morning my brother Chris and I would walk up Gun Club Rd, turn left onto Hollywood Rd and pass Johnson Rd. We would keep walking until Hollywood Rd. merged into Bankhead Highway, which has now been renamed to Donald Lee Hollowell Parkway. We would then cross the street and pass the gas station that sold more alcoholic beverages than actual gas and a Mrs. Winners Fried Chicken restaurant that had the best steak biscuits and cinnamon swirls you'd ever taste. Not the healthiest meal options, but what healthy restaurants have you seen in the hood?

Purpose Over   Pointless Excuses

We finally reached our school, West Fulton Middle School, which has also been renamed to John Lewis Invictus Academy.

For once, that I could remember, I was excited about going to school. Although it was a new school, for the first time I was going to a new school with familiar faces. I, somehow, had managed to make a couple of friends while at Boyd Elementary and we all were at West Fulton together. Even the students that I had not become friends with, I recognized them as some of the same peers from my elementary school. We were *all* new students at this point.

West Fulton Middle School seemed massive in comparison to Boyd Elementary. It sat at the top of a big hill and had kids from other local elementary schools there too. I later found out that it was so big because it was formerly West Fulton High School.

Now here I am, a sixth grader with friends. I was starting to feel a little bit of confidence. I met new people and made more friends. Exciting right? Tell me about it.

One of the new friends I made was a girl named Niki. We actually became best friends. Yeah, Niki and I used to get into trouble often. We were smart students and finished our work early, only to later sit in the classroom being disruptive by talking, eating candy and the pre-sweetened Kool-Aid right out of the pack, waiting for the other students to complete their assignments.

One in-school memory that stayed with me was when our 6th grade teacher caught Niki and I eating Kool-Aid in class. Even though she and I both were eating, *I* got called to the front of the classroom. I tried to lie about the fact that I was eating in class, but the teacher called me out. I am steadily trying to deny eating the FRUIT PUNCH flavored Kool-Aid, not realizing that my mouth, the palm of my left hand and right index finger were red. The evidence was obviously clear; I was guilty. Being the friend she was, Niki quickly put me up on the secret. As I made my walk of shame back to my seat, she whispered, "you need to get the lemonade flavored Kool-Aid because it does not leave a color on you." Genius! Unfortunately, her advice was overheard by the teacher and she got into trouble as well. I think we stopped talking in that lady's class for a few days, but we started right back and continued to eat *lemonade* kool-aid together for the rest of the school year.

I don't remember exactly when or how we started, but my brother Chris and I started walking Niki and her friend, Nichelle, home from school every day. That's until one day in seventh grade I was caught by surprise. My brother and I got home from school and there was a moving truck in the driveway. Not again!

Chris and I had no idea that we were going to be moving. It all happened so suddenly. Here I am, once more, heartbroken, scared, and confused. I had just gotten comfortable, *some* confidence, and now I was forced to become uncomfortable again. We moved from the west side of Atlanta back to the east side of Atlanta to a duplex in the Kirkwood community on a street called Dearborn.

I was enrolled into Sammy E. Coan Middle School; new school, new students, new teachers. AGAIN! I never got the chance to say goodbye to the elementary and middle school friends I had made. I never even got a chance to say goodbye to Niki.

Sammy E. Coan Middle School was in the Edgewood community. Now this middle school was not much different from West Fulton because there were a lot of kids from different neighborhoods going to the same school. The tough part about it was that, just like on the West Side, these kids were mean and tough too. You had kids from Edgewood, East Atlanta, Kirkwood, and East Lake all representing their neighborhoods at the same school. There were food fights in the cafeteria and even neighborhood fights after school. I was the new kid again, so of course I didn't fit in with anyone.

I stayed to myself, until one day my seventh grade teacher, Mr. Ware, had the class to break up into groups for an assignment. The assignment was for us to do some research on a topic and then do a presentation about what we learned in front of the entire class. The thing that made this particular assignment special was that we were able to do the presentation in the form of a song. My group and I did the research together and decided that I would be the voice of the group on presentation day. I soon realized that my teammates were afraid to speak publicly.

Purpose Over   Pointless Excuses

This was perfect! You see, nobody knew that I secretly had a gift for singing and rapping. What they also didn't know was that while back at Boyd Elementary, two of my classmates and I wrote and performed a rap song for our school's black history program. So I even had a little on-stage experience under my belt. This was my big shot.

I remember this day like it was yesterday. My group decided to use the instrumental of a song performed by DJ Taz, Ms. Neeka and Raheem the Dream. DJ Taz was a popular and influential DJ and rapper at that time and the instrumental came from one of his hit songs called "That's Right." What a perfect title and what perfect timing. I finally had an opportunity to do something I was actually good at. THAT'S RIGHT!

So, here we go. It is presentation day and I was ready. I mean, I was "really" ready. The beat dropped, (that means the instrumental started playing) and I stepped out in the middle of the classroom with my group behind me cheering me on. I was in my zone. I opened my mouth and surprised everyone. It was amazing! In fact, it was so amazing that Mr. Ware went next door and told another teacher that she HAD to come see this.

The teacher, Ms. Willams, brought her entire class over to watch us perform the song again. I couldn't believe it. I was being asked to do an encore. I was beyond excited. As you already know, when that beat dropped, it was on! This time I was really feeling it. In that moment, it felt like my confidence went through the roof. I had done it. I had not only earned an A on that assignment for our group, but I had successfully educated and entertained two seventh grade classes and two seventh grade teachers at the same time.

What I didn't understand on that day, was that I was getting a glance at what my true Potential looked like. I had no idea that this would actually serve as a defining moment in my life. In my eyes, I was nothing, a nobody, a complete loser. However, on that particular day, to those teachers and classroom peers, I was smart, I was gifted, I was talented. I was actually somebody special.

It is funny how we can experience moments of greatness and still forget that we have greatness inside of us when life throws us curveballs. It's so easy to fall back into the negative ways of viewing ourselves. We believe the lies to be the TRUTH, especially when the moments of uncertainty and failure seem to significantly outnumber the moments of clarity and success.

My rise to the top didn't last long. I ended up falling face first right back down into my comfort zone. I fell back into what I considered normal; feeling unworthy. Since I thought of myself this way, it appeared that my peers did too. What I did not realize was that they were treating me the same way I was treating myself; poorly. When there were no more hand claps and smiles when I came to school this confirmed what I felt on the inside. Everyone seemed to forget how gifted, how talented, and how special I was. Even me. I was right back where I started. My "fifteen minutes of fame" was over. I was back to being rejected. I was back to being insecure. I was back to being timid and passive. Yes. I was even back to being picked on and bullied. I had gone from worth watching to worthless. This was a self image that would follow me all the way through the eighth grade. Even though I actually had a couple of friends that didn't laugh at me or pick on me, I was not secure in who I was.

   I finally graduated from Coan Middle School. Yep, I did it! I survived six elementary schools, two middle schools and now I was on my way to the big leagues. You see, I was looking forward to going to High School for the same reasons that I was excited about attending West Fulton Middle school; everyone was the new student. Not just me. But then it hit me. Wait, that's... *Nine different schools!!!*

<u>Discovery Moment</u>

Sometimes we can overlook or underestimate defining moments in our lives. Writing this book forced me to think back and recall some of those times. Even while struggling and on my way to my ninth school, there was evidence that I had potential and value but I just didn't see it. Think about where you are in your life right now.

1. How many times have you been the n*ew kid* to a school, neighborhood, team?
2. What are some problems that you have experienced because of it?
3. How did you feel about those experiences and what would you change about them if you could?
4. How many defining moments have you missed or ignored that could be tied into your actual Purpose? Identify them below.

Purpose Over | Pointless Excuses

PURPOSE NOTES

PURPOSE NOTES

Purpose Over — Pointless Excuses

PURPOSE NOTES

CHAPTER 3

ROUGH TRANSITION...

The year was 1998 and High School would prove to be yet another defining moment in my life. The first day of High School was similar to my first day at West Fulton Middle School because I was attending school with most of the same students from Coan Middle School. The fact that there were familiar faces at school made me feel a bit of comfort. However, I had not forgotten that I still wasn't popular or cool like the other kids were. Regardless of what I was thinking or how I felt, one thing I didn't see changing for the next year was the fact that I was now an insecure freshman in high school. To add to this difficult realization, I was not attending any old high school; I was a freshman at Alonzo A. Crim High School. This school had a well known reputation for violence and even had a nickname of "Crime High School."

Crim High School was formerly named Murphy High School and my mom and her siblings went there. For many years, my grandparents had a family home located at 2395 Boulevard Drive, right off of Second Avenue, which was not too far from the East Lake Meadows housing projects. Those housing projects were often referred to as "Little Vietnam." It was called that because of all the violence that was associated with it. During my moms high school days, Murphy High School had another nickname too, "Murder High." From Little Vietnam, to Murder High, to Crime High. Here we go.

Here I was, a second generation Pope in the same neighborhood and same school building as my preceding generation. The reputation of the school was pretty much the same. The only difference was the name. Whether it was called Murphy High, Murder High, Crim High, or Crime High, I was there, still trying to fit in and still trying to find my place. Still trying to be everyone except me and becoming a product of my environment in the process. In fact, I was slowly becoming a product of all of my environments put together.

The thing is, I learned quickly that there was not much of a difference between any of the environments I grew up in. To be honest with you, I had no idea that what I witnessed growing up was actually "traumatizing." I thought it was just your normal everyday drama. Since poverty looked the same in each new neighborhood, school and community, I figured that this was the way everyone lived. I unknowingly normalized abnormal.

Unlike at Coan Middle School, I was fortunate enough to have a big cousin that was a senior at Crim High school during my freshman year. He had a well known reputation for being nice at "throwing them hands," which meant fighting. This cousin was also very popular and well respected. He was on the football team, basketball team, and ran track. When you talk about gifted, he was definitely it and so I had someone else I wanted to be like. I did not feel bad about wanting to be like my big cousin because he was family. He was liked. He was respected. Bottom line, he wasn't me.

I was truly proud to be his little cousin. Although, I had never played any organized sports before, I loved football. As a little kid I used to say that I wanted to be a football player when I grew up. For that reason, I decided to join the Crim High School Football Team like my cousin, but I wasn't very athletic. Compared to some of the other guys on the team who were exceptionally talented, I was often overlooked and my jersey was always the cleanest after every game.

As a freshman football player, there was sort of a hazing ritual that you had to go through at Crim. At least I had to go through it. I remember one day in the locker room, one of the seniors mentioned slapping me to another teammate. What this player did not know was that he was actually saying what he was going to do to me, to my big cousin. My cousin laughed and casually asked him, "Who you talkin' bout slappin?" When the senior pointed at me, he soon regretted it. As you probably guessed by now, things didn't work out so well for that senior on that day. My cousin did not hesitate getting in his face, letting that senior know that I was his "lil cousin" and that he wasn't going to touch me, period. I was astonished at how fast the senior began to apologize and try to make light of the situation.

This was surprising to me because this particular senior my cousin had just threatened was known as one of the most feared and respected guys on the football team. It was in that moment, I realized just how much "juice" my big cousin had. Being his little cousin, man, I felt like I was untouchable. Especially when my big cousin was around. The only thing I found strange was that my cousin always wanted me to do the right thing in high school. He tried to keep me out of trouble even when he, himself, would get into trouble. I remember trying to skip class one day and I ran into him. This was the first and only time he had ever appeared angry at me. He looked at me and asked me what in the "curse word" I was doing cutting class? I was caught off guard because to me, it looked like he was doing the exact same thing. I figured that we could cut class together.

Big Cuz wasted no time firmly telling me to take my "curse word" back to class. This wasn't the only time he would prevent me from making some of the same poor choices he was making. I didn't understand it back then, but now I get it. You want the best for those you care about even if that best does not include you.

As I think back on a *lie challenging* conversation between one of my former classmates from middle school and my big cousin, it was another defining moment in my life. This particular classmate of mine was surprised to hear that my cousin and I were related. I remember him saying to my cousin, "Aye, is this your cousin? Man, your cousin is smart. I'm talkin' bout like a computer bro!" I couldn't believe what I was hearing. This was another popular and respected peer I knew from middle school saying this about me to my big cousin who was also popular and respected in high school. The way the guy said it with such passion forced me to believe that he actually meant what he had just said. Wow! I had no idea that this guy thought so highly of me and for so long. I thought everyone ignored me in middle school! I was literally speechless. Again, I wasn't aware of the fact that this was another glimpse into what my true Potential looked like. I knew I was smart, but thought I was able to hide it so I would not be teased about it, on top of everything else my peers made fun of me about.

   This guy saw right through my act and made it known that day. My big cousin obviously saw something in me too that I didn't recognize in myself. He also recognized my true Potential and that is why he was always on my back, trying to keep me from following in his footsteps.

It's funny how other people can see in you what you either can't see or refuse to see in yourself. It's like the signs were always there to encourage me. Yet, I was still choosing to view myself in a negative way. Although people that already had the respect that I wanted was actually validating me for who I was, I was still trying to be somebody I wasn't. What he said showed me then that it's okay to be smart, gifted and talented. But I never thought so. I was too busy trying to be a follower. The whole time I was supposed to be leading.

Have you ever found yourself trying too hard to be a follower or trying too hard to fit into CIRCLES when you are actually a *STAR*? If so, then I can relate because that was me. I didn't really appreciate my own value. I was completely unaware of my own significance and importance. I believed the lies; worthless, unwanted, rejected. My life and positivity had nothing in common and that was my truth.

At Crim, I had a literature teacher that also taught drama class. This teacher was always respectful to me, so I decided to take drama class too. I really enjoyed acting and being in the stage plays. Believe it or not, people actually liked the characters I played. I guess I had already been acting for years. After all, I was always trying, or better yet *acting* like the cool kids and trying to *act* tougher than I really was. No matter how much I loved drama class and the stage plays, I still wasn't good enough or popular enough to win any accolades though. It's like the same people always got all the hand claps and awards. Not because they were that much more talented, but perhaps because they were just more popular. Perhaps they were doing what I wasn't doing, which was accepting themselves. They knew who they were and didn't need to *act* like anyone else. Even still, knowing this didn't make me feel more confident, but even more insecure because I simply didn't know me.

   Still searching for my place in this gigantic world called high school, I tried all sorts of different things. I even tried and made connections with other people from other schools and neighborhoods. I was drawn to some of these people because they seemed to always have money, nice clothes, shoes and respect. I later found out how they were getting their money. I even found out how they were getting their respect too. Illegally!

To me, it didn't matter how they were getting it. All I knew was that I wanted what they had. I was tired of wearing old hand me down clothes and being poor. I was tired of being picked on. I wanted some money too. I wanted some respect too and now I knew just how I would get it. You see, the guys I had connected with were drug dealers and that's how they got their money for the clothes and shoes they wore. I wasn't new to the drug scene because it was always fluent in my neighborhoods and unfortunately, in my household too. But hanging around these guys, I quickly came to the realization that, not only did they sell drugs, they were gang members too. Their gang affiliation is why they were feared and respected. The interesting thing about it was that they were members of the same gang that my brother and I had secretly joined while we were living on the west side of Atlanta attending West Fulton Middle School.

When we moved away from the west side, we lost contact with those guys. Well, I lost contact with them. My brother,

Chris, had a different story because he was always running the streets; going wherever he wanted to go and doing whatever he wanted to do. I was too afraid of my mom and her *proper forms of persuasion,* as my late Uncle Anthony called it, when I misbehaved, so I stayed home. Don't laugh too hard at me.

The name of the gang will not be mentioned in this book because I am no longer active and I do not wish to promote it or that lifestyle. What I will say is that things definitely started to change for me from that point on. I started making my own money and I started gaining some respect too. The gang became my new family. In that family there were guys called Big Homie. The Big Homie is one who has been in the gang for a while, knows the ins and outs and is respected because of it.

One of the big homies found out that I could not fight and forced me to fight with other members of the gang regularly until he knew I was able to hold my own. Fighting with other guys that were twice my size. Fighting with guys that had been "throwing hands" for years. Guys that could literally punch someone so hard, they would fall asleep instantly. This was my way in and I had to do what I had to do. Some would say that fighting these types of guys everyday was cruel. I would say I finally learned how to fight. I was finally able to defend myself. It was a weird way to learn, but I did. I even had a very large group of people that were willing to fight *for* me too.

One day, out of nowhere, one of my peers decided to try and fight me after school. I don't know the true reason. I can only guess that it was simply because he figured he could easily beat me. What he did not know was that another one of my cousins and a few associates, who were also members of the same gang, were outside waiting for me after school that day.

You see, I was never the big or muscular type, but my cousin was. Some of the other members of the gang were too. All I had to do was say the word and believe it or not, that guy would have never known what hit him. Although I now had the power to get somebody *touched* and the reinforcements to throw my weight around, I could not bring myself to do it. On the inside, I knew back then, I was not that type of person. I was always the merciful and compassionate type. This was probably because I knew how it felt personally to be bullied and beat up. I did not have it in me. Or so I thought....

Along with this newfound knowledge and reinforcements, came a new me. I did not get that one guy from my high school beat up, but I can not say the same for other people after that.

Let's just say that sometimes people and situations can cause you to become someone you were never meant to be. They can even make your heart turn cold at times. There were times where I actually became the bully and the aggressor.

In the midst of all the drama I was now willingly a part of, there was always something inside of me convicting me for my destructive behavior. There was something inside of me saying that I could not continue to purposely cause pain to others for the sake of wanting to fit in. Remember, I was typically the merciful and compassionate type. This was mostly because, although I was growing up in those rough conditions, I was also raised in the church. I was taught better and I definitely knew better. Oftentimes, I'd wonder if growing up in the church was actually the reason why I was not able to fit in and was so passive for so long....? I'm not sure, but I do know that if it had not been for my relationship with God, I don't think I would have survived some of the things I've seen.

The year was 2002 and it was my senior year at Crim High School. Yep, from freshman to senior year, I managed to stay at the same school but things were taking a turn for the worse. After riding the bench on my high school football team most of the season, I was finally called to play. I remember being so excited that I went home screaming to my mom, "Ma, I am playing in the game this Friday night!" I was expecting the same excitement in return but boy was I wrong. "I don't care nothing about no game. You either find a way to bring some money in this house or find somewhere else to stay," she said. My brother-in-law and I made eye contact. I tried to play it off, but he could read in my demeanor that I was ashamed and felt embarrassed. He didn't say anything and neither did I. He just turned around and got into his silver Dodge Ram truck and backed out of the driveway.

Purpose Over   Pointless Excuses

I still played in the game that Friday night, but by Sunday, while my mom was at church, I packed all of my clothes in trash bags, piled them up on the side of the house and left the only home I knew. I couldn't believe that at 17 years old I could no longer be a typical high school student, but someone that had to find a better paying job and somewhere to L.I.V.E.

I had no idea where I was going or what I was going to do next. I just began walking with the clothes on my back and about $300 dollars worth of crack in my pocket. All of the clothes I packed in trash bags were still on the side of my house and I was praying that they would still be there when I got back. I was so hurt and confused. After a long while of walking in a daze, I ended up at my cousin, Eric's, house. My cousin Eric, or Big E as everyone called him is a true family man. He didn't take mess from anyone and spoke his mind about what he felt was right.

On this day though, he took me right back home. I was still disappointed so I stayed outside while Big E and his wife, Rena, went inside to talk with my mom. I don't know what was said, but when they came outside, Big E said that

Purpose Over Pointless Excuses

I could come with them, so I grabbed my bags and put them in the back of their van. When we got back to their home, Big E showed me where I could sleep and where I could put my clothes.

While unpacking, all of the $300 dollars worth of crack fell out of my pockets. My heart stopped. Big E took a deep breath, looked me in the eye and lifted his hand. I flenched thinking that the physical abuse from my younger years was about to repeat itself. However, he placed his hand on my shoulder and gave me a "man to man" talk. "I understand your circumstances and the environment that you come from. I am not telling you what to do or not to do and you are more than welcome to crash here, but you have to respect my house and my family." Those were some of the realest words I had ever heard from a man at that time, which is why, in my heart, I knew I could never sell crack while living under his roof. I went to the bathroom and flushed every bit of crack I had on me down the toilet. That night I couldn't fall asleep right away. I stayed up thinking about all that happened; what my mom said to me, what Big E said to me, respect, what I did, where I was and how my life was changing so suddenly. Next thing I knew the alarm clock was going off because it was time for me to go to school. Since I now lived further away from my school, I had to get up earlier. Away from home, no money, crack gone. Man! What a *rough transition*!

Around homecoming time, I was running for the position of *Mr. Crim High School*. I didn't really want to run for the position, but my counselor and my assistant principal talked me into it. So there I was, waiting for my turn to give my speech. This would be my first time actually speaking publicly, unless you count that one time back in seventh grade during the *That's Right* presentation or the Black History program back in fifth grade. What made this time so different was that there was no music with this presentation. It was not a song, it was a speech and there was no one responsible for the outcome but me. The gym was jammed packed with the entire school population. It is my turn to give my speech. Here I go! I stepped up to the microphone and nervously gave the quick campaign speech I had prepared. Take a guess at what happened. Go on, I'll wait. Now let's see if you guessed correctly. The entire gym erupted! All I could hear was the loud thunderous sound of BOOING! I couldn't believe what was happening to me. It was like I was having a nightmare, but I was wide awake, so this was real. I was heartbroken, embarrassed, and ultimately rejected. I was shown no mercy and no compassion. I wanted to run and hide, but there was no place I could hide because everyone had witnessed or participated in my demise.

Talk about a bad day. In spite of the pain and shame I was feeling, I had to stand there and take it as every other candidate received welcoming cheers and applause. This was the day it was confirmed that I was not accepted or respected by the majority of my high school peers.

Although I felt a hurt so deep that day, this was yet another defining moment in my life. I didn't realize it at the time, but that day actually gave me a courage that I didn't know I had. From that moment on, I was no longer afraid to pick up a microphone and stand on a stage in public. As a matter of fact, research shows that the number one fear for about 98% of the people on the planet is actually Public Speaking.

Thanks to that day, I had already experienced the worst case scenario and already survived what 98% of the world's population fear the most. Although I still get nervous, I'm definitely no longer afraid.

I went on from that day to actually be voted "Most Talented" by my peers in our Senior Class Yearbook. Who knew? All those times I did not get a round of applause during the stage plays. That time I got booed. Those times I got bullied; my talent was still recognized. I was even selected to sing at our High School Graduation that was held at the Civic Center in Atlanta, GA.

I was finally starting to learn that tests and trials come not to break us, but to actually make us. That is, if we allow the growth process to take place.

Discovery Moment

Throughout my entire childhood, I was constantly trying to avoid facing my fears and insecurities. I was always trying to hide or cover up who I was, my intellect, or my talent. I was constantly living up to the lies my situations lead me to believe. I was trying so hard to run from the rejection, I ended up running right into it almost everywhere I went. Little did I know, the rejection, the abandonment, the bullying and all the suffering I had endured was making me stronger mentally. I was actually "growing" through all of the pain and hurt I was experiencing. It wasn't happening *to me*, it was happening *for me*.

1. What struggles can you relate to from this chapter?
2. What emotions did you feel while reflecting and writing down those struggles?
3. Do you know others that are experiencing similar struggles? How would you encourage them?
4. What are some things you would have done differently if the main character in this chapter was you?

Purpose Over — Pointless Excuses

PURPOSE NOTES

PURPOSE NOTES

Purpose Over Pointless Excuses

PURPOSE NOTES

Purpose Over Pointless Excuses

CHAPTER 4

IDENTITY CRISIS...

Purpose Over Pointless Excuses

Not only did I get kicked out when I was 17 years old, or so I thought, but I had another life changing moment soon after graduation.

One night I went with one of my cousins to a drug deal that went bad. I no longer sold crack at this time but I was selling weed. I can't remember if the guy was my cousin's former cell mate or just a guy that was locked up in the same cell block. Anyway, the guy shows up to pick my cousin up which to me was odd, but whatever. As my cousin is about to hop in the car, I noticed that there was someone in the passenger seat of the car too. At this point I'm thinking, I can't let cuz go solo, so I jump in the car with them. The driver, who my cousin knew from jail, pulls off. I don't recall the exact time, but I do remember that it was dark. He made a right turn out of the apartment complex onto the main road. We stopped at the first red light and the passenger who hasn't said a word the whole time, takes another pull from the blunt he fired up as soon as we got in the car. He took a long pause before blowing a big cloud of smoke up towards the roof of the small car we were in. He then reaches over his shoulder to pass me the blunt. Of course, I rejected it. I may be a lot of things, but someone that shares a blunt with a person I don't know or didn't see roll beforehand is a non-negotiable.

I looked at him and said "I'm good, but 'preciate it," while thinking to myself, ain't no way. I don't know you and I didn't see you roll it. His response was, "You sure?" I nodded. He pointed the blunt towards my cousin who gladly accepted. I gave my cousin a slight nudge with my right elbow and tried to tell him not to hit the blunt. I think the driver saw me because when I looked up, I could have sworn he was looking right at me. He didn't say anything. He just kind of locked eyes with his partner in crime who was trying his best not to look too obvious.

My cousin is hitting the blunt so hard, he hasn't noticed a thing. By this time, we are making a right turn into another apartment complex. We travel down a small hill and the driver parks the car. We all get out the car and a third guy walks up out of, what seemed to be, no where. He tells me that only one of us can come inside and that's the person doing the business. My cousin and I looked at one another. Then he said, "It's cool cuz, don't trip. I'll be right back." At this point I'm like, "You sure cuz?" He loudly reassured me with, "CUZ, I'M GOOD!"

Now I am standing beside the car as my cousin walks down stairs with his friend from jail and the third random guy who just appeared out of no where. Oh yeah, the guy on the passenger side had gotten back in the car and was just sitting there with his door open. My gut was telling me that something was wrong, but my cuz said that he was good, so I stayed where I was. A few moments later, things took a turn for the worst. It was already as dark as when you close your eyes and we were in some apartments that neither of us lived around. Then it happened. I found myself starring down the barrel of a loaded 12 gauge shot gun.

Instantly, my life began to flash before my eyes. For a quick couple of seconds, I couldn't even hear all the yelling and screaming the robbers were doing. It all happened so fast that there was no time to even reach for a weapon. We were then told to turn around and start walking towards the woods in the back of the apartments. My cousin and I looked at each other. Right then I could have sworn the guy

Purpose Over Pointless Excuses

with the 12 gauge pulled the trigger. In my opinion, it's only by the grace of GOD that the gun didn't go off but we didn't give him a second chance to pull the trigger again, as we both ran like our lives depended on it because at that moment, it did. Then all of a sudden, just as fast as it had started, it was over. I was still alive, unharmed and so was my cousin. Now that's what I call a Miracle! That night I realized that I was at a fork in the road and I had to really decide whether to continue down the path I was traveling or to make some major changes in my life. After all, I literally could have been killed. It took some time for me to get my head together after that, but one thing I knew for sure was that I had more learning to do, but I needed to figure who I really was. Fast.

   I didn't like me. I didn't want to be me. I felt broken and worthless. I felt abandoned and rejected by my biological father. I was even unsure of the identity of my biological father because he told me himself that I wasn't his son. I felt like Demont was a nobody. You see, Demont was timid and passive. Demont was bullied and pushed around. Demont wasn't as tough as his brothers. Demont wasn't cool like the other kids. He felt like he couldn't do much of anything right. He tried to play sports, but wasn't athletic enough. He tried to be a ladies man but couldn't keep track of what lie he told and which girl he told it to. He tried to be a gangster, but his heart was too big. He tried selling drugs, but cared too much about the drug addicts. He tried to be a goody two shoe church boy, but wasn't holy enough, so he always felt like a hypocrite. All lies!!!

I slowed my life down and started to focus on me more than my surroundings. I then noticed that the only thing that brought me comfort and happiness over the years was music.

I remember the first time I heard a song by Tupac Shakur (My Favorite Rapper). In that song, he wasn't rapping about money, drugs, sex or violence. Instead, he was actually telling young people that there was more to life than all of those things. He said "You can be an accountant, not a dope dealer, instead of out here pimping, you can be an attorney like Johnnie Cochran." If you don't know who that is, he's the Attorney that was famous for representing the former pro football player, OJ Simpson during his high profile murder trial. After hearing those words from Tupac, I decided to try to try to write songs too. I now wanted to become a rapper. I also rediscovered my love for singing, so I started doing it more and writing R&B songs. I knew I was not good at being a gangster or a ladies man. So, being a gangster rapper or R&B singer didn't fit me very well. The fact that I was raised in church and in the ghetto at the same time, led me to rap and sing about that.

I came up with the acronym, G.Y.N.E.S.I.S (God's Youth Need Education So I Speak) and started a rap duo with my cousin, Dante, called 2BLESSED. We would make music that l called GHETTO GOSPOL, which was another acronym that meant "Going Hard Everyday Trying To Give Our Savior Praises Out Loud." Now during this time, Gospel Rapping wasn't considered cool or popular but neither was I, so it seemed a perfect fit for me. What I realized ended up blowing my mind. I discovered that people actually liked G.Y.N.E.S.I.S. He was respected and people thought he was cool, so I took pride in that name and identity. I felt like that name was valuable and significant. I even found out that girls liked him too. He was everything that I wished Demont could be.

As 2BLESSED, we were on our way to being what we considered successful. We were performing any and everywhere we could. Because of our hard word and determination, we ended up with a Manager and also a Sponsor who would give us clothes to wear at our performances. We even got the opportunity to open in concert for Gospel music icon John P. Kee, who is a highly decorated and notable gospel singer and pastor. What happened next, would strike a devastating blow right to the heart of 2BLESSED.

One morning, I got a phone call from my cousin, Eric, stating that Dante was in the hospital because he had gotten into a car accident while fleeing from the police. I couldn't believe what I was hearing. My cousin, best friend, and business partner all in one, was in major trouble. I was in disbelief and denial. Most of the time, Dante and I went everywhere and did everything together. This time, I wasn't there and I was furious with myself because of it. I was devastated because I felt like I had let my cousin and best friend down. I was not even thinking about the fact that I would have probably been in the exact same situation if I *had* been there. I don't know for sure if I could have or even would have been able to do anything to change the outcome of that situation, but I felt guilty about not being there anyway.

Dante ended up being sentenced to 10 years in prison after he got out of the hospital and my heart was completely shattered into pieces. I was alone again and our Duo, 2BLESSED, was dead. I couldn't do anything to help Dante get out of prison, but I wanted to seek revenge on the so called friends I felt was responsible for putting him in there.

During a phone conversation with Dante one day, I talked about seeking revenge on those guys, not caring one bit that I was on a recorded line. I had it mapped out and was letting my cousin know that I had his back. However, my mind was blown. Again. Dante asked me to make him a promise that I didn't want to keep. He asked me not to retaliate on our former "friends" because he did not want me to be sharing a prison cell with him. He said that our family was hurting enough and that they did not need to lose me to prison too. Imagine that. Here my cousin was, at the lowest point in his life and was still more concerned about others than himself.

In that moment, I learned that you can let yourself down often and not think twice about it. It becomes a different story when you consider not letting others down. It was very difficult, to say the least, but thanks be to GOD, I was able to keep that promise. It was one of the hardest promises I'd ever have to keep, but I would *not* let him down.

Discovery Moment

It's hard being young and trying to find your place in this gigantic world. With so many different influencers and influences constantly battling for your attention, it is very possible to find yourself suffering from an identity crisis. Especially when you come from a broken home or a dysfunctional family. Trying so hard to fit into a life you think you want could potentially lead to you losing yourself or your life completely.

1. What are some problems that may cause a person to have an Identity Crisis?
2. When was the last time you felt like you were struggling to find your identity?
3. What are some ways that can help a person avoid an identity crisis?
4. What are you going to do, starting now, to secure your identity?

PURPOSE NOTES

PURPOSE NOTES

PURPOSE NOTES

Chapter 5

MINDSET SHIFT...

Purpose Over Pointless Excuses

A year after graduating from high school, I went to live with my older sister, Shan. The year was 2003. I was legally an adult and desperate to become my own man. My big sister had always been there for me throughout my childhood. She was actually the only way that I received what cool looking name brand clothes I did have to wear to school as a kid.

She would pick me up during the summer breaks and take me back to Florida with her and her family. This meant the world to me because it gave me the only escape I had from my "normal" environment.

At the time, Shan's husband, my brother in law, was still in the U.S. Navy. I admired him and his brothers because they were all in the military and to me, they were real heroes. They each had a wife or girlfriend, which made them seem even cooler; family men. So one day, after talking with my brother in law and his twin brother, I made one of the biggest decisions of my life. That's right, you guessed it! I decided to join the military too. After all, I did do very well in high school JROTC and I wanted to be my own man.

Purpose Over   Pointless Excuses

That next week following our conversation, I spoke with a recruiter and did the unthinkable for someone like me. Although I was insecure, timid, and passive, I did it. I enlisted in the United States Armed Forces. Soon afterwards, I was at the Military Entrance Processing Station aka MEPS, ready to go. I was tired of being soft and scary, so I did something bold and courageous for myself and for the first time, by myself. No big sister, big brother, big cousin, or my mom to be with me. I was completely alone.

From MEPS, the next thing I knew, I was in a van on my way to a hotel with other newly enlisted kids and scheduled to fly out to Basic Training early the very next morning. When I woke up that morning though, I was terrified. I couldn't believe what I had done, but I could not take it back. I was on my way to Lackland Air Force Base in San Antonio, Texas. The only time I had been away from home was when I went to spend the summer in Jacksonville, Florida with Shan. Now I was on my way to San Antonio Texas. I was all alone. Well, except for one other guy from Atlanta whose last name was Bernard.

Bernard and I got along well and became friends. Before arriving to San Antonio, our flight stopped in Dallas, Texas. We were supposed to take a second flight to San Antonio, but we both thought that a layover meant that we were supposed to spend the night in Dallas. Two young men from Atlanta, Georgia who had never been too far from home, much less on an airplane unaccompanied, we were clueless. So we literally *laid over*.

Stop judging me!

Perhaps you can see why Bernard and I got along so well. Neither of us were the sharpest tools in the shed, if you know what I mean.

Our ignorance would prove to be a BIG mistake, as the next day we were supposed to be in San Antonio for Basic Training, but guess where we were? That's right, we were still in Dallas. We managed to get in touch with someone back at the MEPS who informed us of how bad we had screwed up. We then received new plane tickets from Dallas to San Antonio. When we finally arrived in San Antonio, there was a van waiting for us and the driver, who was also in the Air Force, drove us straight to Lackland Air Force Base without any small talk at all.

It was a very unpleasant and uncomfortable ride. Bernard and I had no idea what we were in for. Here we were arriving to Basic Training or "Boot Camp"as some called it, an entire day late. We were met outside of a building by a tall dark man wearing a big hat. He was in uniform and had a name tag that said Banks. He had stripes on his shoulder identifying him as a Technical Sergeant or "TSgt". He, too, did not seem happy to meet us. He immediately began screaming and yelling at us. TSgt. Banks was commanding us to get into the building, rushing us up several flights of stairs and through a large metal door. When we got inside the door, there was another man who appeared to be Hispanic. This guy was dressed exactly like TSgt Banks, but his name tag said Martinez and the stripes on his shoulder identified him as a Staff Sergeant or "SSgt" for short. This guy was just as aggressive and loud as TSgt Banks was.

Neither of them seemed nice or friendly at all. What made it even worse was that there were about fifty other trainees in this room and they were all being yelled at and doing push-ups too. What did I sign up for?

I could tell some form of physical activity had been going on for a while by the smell of sweat and musk in the room. It smelled like my high school locker room after game day. Not to mention that the small window on the door seemed to be sweating too. This was surely that moment where I felt like I had made the biggest mistake of my life.

Bernard and I were immediately ordered to join the other guys in the push-up position. Of course, without hesitation, Bernard and I joined in, since we had delayed enough. I noticed that SSgt Martinez was watching the entire group of us as he yelled out "UP....DOWN! UP....DOWN!" Maybe I was mistaken, but it seemed like the more some people cheated the push ups, that is to say people were not going all the way up or down, the more push ups he added on. Me realizing this, but not thinking, I yelled out to motivate everyone," COME ON YALL. STOP TRYING TO CHEAT. YALL MAKING EVERYBODY HAVE TO SUFFER!" The nerve of me. Here I am, a day late, just arriving to the physical activities taking place and yelling at folks! Like I said, not the sharpest tool.

Following my outburst, SSGT Martinez called me to the front of the room. I got up and ran to the front and said what I was required to say, "Sir, Trainee Pope reports as ordered." He then looked at me and ordered me to "About Face" which is to make a 180 degree turn and face the opposite direction. As I looked at the group still in the push-up position, I just knew that I was about to be humiliated in a major way for yelling out at everyone. As I took a deep breath and prepared for the worst, the strangest thing happened. SSGT Martinez told the entire group, "from this day forward, if Pope tells you to do anything, you'd better treat it as if I had said it to you myself." I could not believe my ears. Then I was ordered to "About Face" again. Now I was looking back at SSGT Martinez. The words he spoke next taught me something that I would never forget. He said "leading is not about telling people what to do, it's about setting an example for them to follow. Never order someone to do something that you are not willing or able to do yourself. So, if you order the group to do fifty pushups, they would have to do it, but you better beat them to number fifty. If you ordered them to run a mile, then you'd better lead the way." I quickly answered back with a loud "YES SIR!"

I was stunned. I wasn't getting humiliated. I was actually getting promoted. I was being placed in a leadership position over fifty plus other men. My first thought was that this guy has no idea what kind of mistake he is making. He has no idea who I really am. I'm thinking, "what is going on here?" I had so many other thoughts and questions running through my head with no time to deal with them.

I was not sure that I could do this. I was not sure that I could be a leader. Here I was, after all I had experienced in my childhood, in a leadership role. I had just been made "Dorm Chief".

I thought back to all those times I had been rejected, picked on, and bullied. I wanted to back out of this position, but something on the inside of me wouldn't allow me to speak another word.

This was yet another defining moment in my life. What happened next would prove that I had not made a mistake, but one of the best decisions in my life. As time went by, I not only got stronger physically, but I also gained more confidence too. I endured training that I never ever would've tried on my own. I conquered all sorts of fears. I even gained respect from the other Training Instructors in Basic Training, as well as my entire group of peers.

This feeling was comparable to none I had ever felt before.

On the day that I graduated Basic Training, I took my mom to the dorm to show her where I had been living. As I packed the rest of my belongings, I overheard a conversation that SSGT Martinez was having with my mom. Yet again, I couldn't believe what I was hearing. He told my mom that he hated to see me go. He even said that he wished he had 100 more men like me and that I was a natural born leader. After hearing that, I had to fight off all kinds of emotions. This was definitely the nicest thing I had ever heard SSGT Martinez say. Not only that, but it was also one of the most inspiring things that I had ever heard anyone say about me.

Then, it happened. I finally had that complete *"Mindset Shift."* I told myself that I could do more and I could be more. I couldn't show the emotions that I felt because after all, I was now officially an "Airmen" in the United States Air Force and had been trained to control my emotions and show no weakness. But talk about an eye opening experience.

After basic training was Technical Training or "Tech School" as we called it. This is where I would experience an in-depth training for my specific career field, which was "Security Forces". Imagine that, from insecure, timid, and passive, to one of the most aggressive and physical career fields in the Air Force. I was definitely not the same kid I was when I first entered basic training. Demont was actually becoming a man and a respected member of the world's most powerful military. What was really surprising to me is that my leadership training and role did not end in basic training. It actually continued. I went from being a Dorm Chief over about fifty three men to a "Squadron Yellow Rope," which meant that while at Tech School, I was over about one hundred and twenty other men and women that were also in training. This was pivotal because some of these men and women had prior service experience in other branches of the military such as Army, Navy, and Marines. But here I was supervising *them!*

I learned how to correctly supervise and lead a large group of people that were from various walks of life. I learned that leadership was not all about doing everything myself. I learned how to delegate authority and responsibilities. This meant identifying others with leadership abilities and sharing the overall responsibility of leading the group with them. I was told to select three "Green Ropes" that would receive instructions from me and assist me with making sure that the other one hundred and twenty men and women under our leadership were in compliance.

This went on for a while and then something changed. I went from squadron yellow rope to squadron "Red Rope". This was the most significant thing that happened to me while at Tech School. This was not just a promotion to me. This was a promotion to the highest leadership position that could be held by an airmen in training at Tech School.

This responsibility was far greater than anything else I had experienced so far. Now I was the head airmen in training on the entire military base. I would be receiving my orders directly from the sergeants that were on duty. I would then give those orders to all of the other yellow ropes and they would pass the orders down to their green ropes.

To me this was nothing short of being amazing. What made this moment so monumental for me was that there was a significantly higher number of airmen training on that base at this time than the number of airmen in "boot camp."

Now imagine me, being the head airmen out of all the hundreds of other people who were also in training. I had lived everyday of my life being a follower, not realizing I was a natural born leader. That may be why I didn't fit in. I wasn't supposed to.

Leading several hundred airmen was my reality everyday until I received my orders to report to my duty station. This would be the location I called home while I served on active duty. Do you care to take a wild guess at where I was stationed? Just kidding, I'll tell you. I would spend my short military career at Elmendorf Air Force Base in Anchorage, Alaska. That's right, the kid from Atlanta, Georgia was now a resident of Alaska. It would be there that I would experience my first and only deployment.

  I received a call from my leadership ordering me to quickly pack and prepare to be deployed to an undisclosed location for a mission that I cannot discuss details about to this day. The deployment was a TDY assignment which meant temporary duty. It became even more real. Me. An Airmen that had completed real training during active war time and now I was on my way to carry out a real mission on a real deployment. Other than the fact that the mission was successful, that is all I am at liberty to comment about related to the assignment. But, what I will say is that my life had drastic made an "About Face". Pun definitely intended.

Discovery Moment

I am writing this book because I want you to know that it is possible to step out of INSECURITY and to step INTO the SECURITY of who you are and who you are meant to be. You see, there is power in who you are. As a matter of fact, there is power in your name. I didn't always realize the power of who I was or the significance of my name. As a matter of fact I was ashamed of who I was because I was so insecure. I didn't value my name because, to me, it wasn't valuable until I had that Mindset Shift.

1. When were 3 moments you chose or will choose to confront your fear of?
2. What was it that gave you the courage to face each of those moments?
3. How did you feel about yourself after conquering those fears?
4. What are some some things that you are going to start doing now that will improve your mindset?

PURPOSE NOTES

PURPOSE NOTES

PURPOSE NOTES

CHAPTER 6

CONSISTENCY...

Purpose Over Pointless Excuses

Think about it for a moment, will you. My life started out heading in one direction. The early stages of my childhood began with the death of my twin sister. Then, I was abandoned by my father who was an abusive alcoholic. As if that wasn't tough enough, I ended up with a stepfather that was addicted to crack cocaine and was also verbally abusive to me (we'll talk more about him in Part 2). I grew up in drug and crime infested communities and had to relocate so often that by ninth grade, I was at my ninth school. I was picked on and bullied. I was booed in front of my entire High School. I ended up joining a gang and becoming a drug dealer. I was literally becoming a product of my environment. That direction was destructive.

Everywhere I turned, there was addiction, violence, sadness, and depression. I had every excuse to stay in that same condition. I was tossed to the side, broken, rejected, and felt worthless. I was a complete loser, or so I thought.

In the midst of all the turmoil in my life, I did manage to develop a relationship with GOD. I believe to this day that it was that spiritual relationship that gave me the strength and ability to endure all of the hardships I have managed to survive. Let me remind you that I was raised in church just as much as I was raised in the ghetto. Therefore, there was always a struggle with identity. Am I what I'm learning from church or am I what I'm learning in the streets? These are questions that always seemed to be in my mind. The truth is that I was being molded and shaped by both realities. What really made the difference for me is that I had to reach a point in my life where I was able to decide. Yes, I had to make a decision whether I was going to keep allowing things to happen to me or start making things happen for me.

Perhaps you may be in a similar position. You may be struggling to make a difficult decision. You may be struggling with having to overcome something in your own life. You may be facing a situation right now that seems impossible for you to make it out of. That struggle may be something similar to what I was dealing with or it may be something completely different. That's okay.

I don't claim to know all of the answers to every problem. I don't even claim to be an expert on problem solving. What I do know is that there is always a solution to every problem. In the words of my favorite rapper, Tupac Shakur, "Through every dark night, there's a bright day after that." Now you may be thinking to yourself that there is no way out for you. You may even be feeling a bit hopeless and trapped. What statistics say about people like you, growing up the way you do, having been talked about the way you've been, looking the way you do, having experienced what you have, you aren't worthy. If statistics says you aren't worthy, then it must be true, so why bother trying to change? Right?

Well, I want you to know that I understand exactly how you feel. Honestly, I get it, but I also want you to know that situations nor feelings don't always tell you what's real. Sometimes feelings can exaggerate the truth a bit. Feelings can take you on all sorts of emotional roller coaster rides. They can have you up one minute and down the next. They can have you twisting and turning before you even get a chance to notice it. What we must do is grab a hold of our emotions and make every attempt to control our feelings whenever possible. When you feel overwhelmed, there is nothing wrong with simply stopping. Take a moment for

Purpose Over Pointless Excuses

yourself and breathe. Take a deep breath and relax your mind. This will give you the ability to think clearly.

It's hard to make right decisions when your mind is clouded by distractions and illusions. In fact, it's almost impossible to truly see. A clear thinking mind will give you a *"clearer vision"* of what's in front of you or what you need to do next. This is very important in order for you to make the transition from where you are to where you want or need to be. If you can't see what's in front of you, then how do you expect to travel from one point to your destination?

Another thing we must do is pay attention to our direction. Now, I understand why the windshield in vehicles are so much larger than the rear view mirror. This means that we should not be focusing on what's behind us if we are trying to obtain what is in front of us. Do not allow negative memories to block your vision. Sometimes we waste too much time thinking about what we have been through that it prevents us from making progress towards where we are meant to be. One thing I have learned is that we really are what we think. If we are constantly thinking about the problems that we've faced or are currently facing, then we literally will become or remain those problems. Therefore, it is critical that we begin to think more about the *solutions* to our problems or overcoming whatever it is that we are struggling with.

First thing you should do is stop claiming it. Stop saying my problem. Try saying "the problem" instead. You aren't a problem. It is. Then write it or them all down. Now consider different steps it would take to get out of or get rid of the problem. Write those down too.

Really imagine what it will look like and feel like to be free of the problem. It may seem huge; impossible even, but how do you eat your favorite cake or pie? One bite at a time. Bite by bite, place one foot in front of the other, take it one second at a time. That mode of thinking will give you the ability to move and see past the issues, the problems.

Now that we can see more, we can be more. I also found that all of the great lessons I've learned means absolutely nothing without consistency. If I'm not consistently working on the solution, even when I'm tired or it doesn't feel good, I'll NEVER MAKE IT. Stay consistent. You remember those different steps you wrote down? Well, those can be used as a roadmap of consistent things you can do to reach a solution.

Some may ask, "what if the problem is the death of someone close to me? I can't bring them back. So what can I do?"

You continue to be consistent in your pursuit of honoring them, their memory, and becoming the best You.

Losing my twin, classmates, friends and other loved ones along the way could have paralyzed me. It may be paralyzing to you, but how does you being stuck help anyone? Including yourself and those still alive who needs you?

Grief is a pain that isn't visible. You can't get stitches or put a bandage over it, but it hurts and leaves a scar just the same. Sometimes the pain is a dull ache and sometimes it's a strong force to endure, but stay *consistent* for YOU. Make them proud of the person you are. Become who you are destined to be. Reach your goals. Use that pain to push you toward your purpose. Your life deserves you to live it. Now stay consistent and do it!

Discovery Moment

Keep moving in the direction that is helpful for your life and honorable to those you love. You owe you to see past the lies, to become the best version of yourself.

Again, one bite, one step, one day, one hour, one minute, one second at a time; Consistency!

1. Think about a time your feelings got the best of and you lost control of your emotions. What problems occurred because of it?
2. How did you respond to the problem or problems?
3. How different would your life be if you were free of your problems?
4. What are you going to do, consistently, starting now, to help you identify your purpose even if the problems are still there?

PURPOSE NOTES

Purpose Over — Pointless Excuses

PURPOSE NOTES

Purpose Over   Pointless Excuses

PURPOSE NOTES

CHAPTER 7

FIVE STEPS...

I am excited about the next part of this book and you should be excited too. Not only are we approaching the end, but here is where you get the opportunity to be hands on. This is where you get to practice five simple steps that will help you realize your true Potential and Self-Worth. It's one thing to read this autobiography, it's something entirely different to actually apply the lessons in this book to your everyday lifestyle. I encourage you to write these five steps down if you haven't been taking notes already. Let's go!

STEP 1

The first step I want you to remember is BELIEVE.

Say the word BELIEVE! That's right. You've got to believe. You must first believe that you are not an accident. You have to believe that you are beautifully and wonderfully made. You have to believe that you were created with a Purpose and that you can achieve that purpose.

Did you know that there is a part of the brain that determines what information is important? It's sort of like the internet. Once you search for something you like, the internet thinks it's important to you and will continue to show you similar things based on what you've searched for, what it thought was important. Well, this is what that part of the brain does. It's called the Reticular Activating System (RAS).

Therefore, if your mind is focused on the negative, then the RAS thinks that it must be important to you and will continue to show you negative things. This is why change must start in the mind. You have to make up your mind, *Mindset Shift*, and know that your purpose is bigger than lies and excuses. This will help your INNER ME become stronger than the ENEMY. *BELIEVE* me!

STEP 2

The second step is BE TRUE.

Say the words Be TRUE! Yes, you must be true to yourself. You have to be true to your own purpose and your own values. Often times we feel pressured to be what others want us to be and do what others want us to do. Be True to what you want to accomplish in your life. Be true to what gives you fulfillment. This is accomplished, again, in the mind. If you believe that you're not worthy, you're not valued, you are undeserving, then everything you hear or see from that point will confirm it.

I couldn't be upset with my peers for treating me poorly. I taught them how to do it because I was doing it to myself! I was not being TRUE to who I was. I did all that acting, for what? I still struggled. So instead of wasting time being someone you're not for the sake of others, be True to you. Those who appreciate the real you will stick around. Trust me. Make up in your mind that you're going to be true to yourself and do something positive to impact the world and your world too. Being true to yourself is a freedom like none other!! See for yourself.

STEP 3

The third step is BE STRONG.

Say the words Be STRONG! You got it.

You have to be strong. Not just physically strong but also Mentally Strong. Physical strength is cool, but Mental strength is ice cold. Mental strength gives you the ability to endure and push through when life hits you with all kinds of obstacles and adversity. It's not a matter of if, it's a matter of when. Understand that in this life you *will* face opposition and problems. It's how you respond to the adversity, problems and opposition that makes the difference. Grip that mental barbell and get those mental *reps* in often because adversity is coming, but you're mentally stronger than you realize!

STEP 4

The fourth step I need you to remember is BE YOU.

That's it. Say Be YOU! I read a famous quote by Oscar Wilde that said "Be yourself, everyone else is already taken".

Quick question, how will the rest of the world find you when they come looking for the real you if you're too busy being someone you are not? There are a lot of copies in the world. What the world needs is an original. The world needs you. Not a watered down version of you, but the best version of you. There is only one way to guarantee that you are giving the world your best you; that is to truly and fully embrace your authentic self. This is very important because the *best you* will always be the *real you*.

If you don't know who you are yet, that's okay. But take the time to get to know you sooner than later to avoid the mistakes I made.

What do you like, what don't you like, what makes you happy, sad? What gives you peace and joy outside of money, people, places or things?

It's not selfish for you to take care of yourself or to learn more about you first. How can you pour into the cups of those you care about, if your jug is empty? Get to know you so you can actually BE YOU!

Purpose Over Pointless Excuses

STEP 5
JUST BE

The fifth and final step in this process is to just BE. Say BE!

This is the easiest and yet most important step. This is where you get to actually be whatever it is that you believe you were created and called to be. The one that isn't like anyone else. The one created to make a difference.

All of your life, decisions were made for you; who your family is, what preschool, elementary school, middle school or high school you have to attend. What time you have to be there or what you can and can't wear to certain places.

You don't get many opportunities to just Be. But right here, right now, you can decide. I'm telling you this, you do get to *Be* that Doctor. Be that Lawyer. Be that Judge. Be that Policeman. Be that Fireman. Be that Author. Be that Athlete.

Be that Teacher. Be that Principal. Be that Business Owner. Be that CEO. Be the First person in your family to Graduate High School. Be the First person in your family to Graduate College. Be that Husband. Be that Wife. Be that Father that you never had. Be that Mother that you never had. Be that Designer. Be that Architect. Be that Engineer. Be that Technician. Be that Congressman. Be that Senator. Be that Governor. Be the next President of the United States of America. Be that Speaker. Be that change this world needs. Make up your mind to JUST BE!

Discovery Moment

There are going to be many obstacles and distractions along this journey of Purpose but you have exactly what it takes to be great. The opportunity here is for you to truly decide who you are going to be and not just follow the influence of others. Notice that I said "Opportunity." Now that you know where to start, let's build.

1. What's the biggest dream that you could imagine yourself accomplishing?
2. What talents do you have that you are good at?
3. If money was not an issue for you, what would you enjoy doing everyday?
4. What are you going to start doing now to become who you want to be later?

Purpose Over Pointless Excuses

PURPOSE NOTES

PURPOSE NOTES

Purpose Over   Pointless Excuses

PURPOSE NOTES

CHAPTER 8
~~PERMISSION~~
PURPOSE GRANTED!

Purpose Over Pointless Excuses

I am giving you the permission to step out of insecurity and step into the security of your authentic self. You now have the "Power To Overcome." Now you understand that you do have a PURPOSE. You also know that there is even a purpose for that struggle. You also know now that you can and will OVERcome the pain. You are not stronger *in spite of* the heartache, the lack, the rejection, the low self-value.

You are stronger *because of it*. You now know that it is POINTLESS to worry about the past and things that you can not control. Like I've said before, you can't control who your family is, when you're born, where you live as a child, or most times, what age you will be when you leave this earth. So, why continue to stress about things or a beginning you have no control over? You have been granted the permission to release it. Your purpose demands it!

Average people choose to make EXCUSES about why their life is unsuccessful. Not you. You are above average because you will choose to find or create a way to make your life a success. You now have permission to go be YOU on PURPOSE!

Until we meet again, just know that I believe in you. I believe you have what it takes to change your world. I want you to know that I love you and I will tell you more about my journey when we meet again in my next book. See you in Part Two!

TO BE CONTINUED... IN BOOK 2

Discovery Moment

Congratulations to you for completing this book. I am grateful that you took time to read the first part of my journey of becoming DEMONT POPE and *how I discovered the power to overcome,* ignore the lies and just BE. I hope you took notes or highlighted some areas to refer back to when life starts lying on you or to you again about your Purpose.

1. What are three areas of this book that spoke to you the most?
2. What are some things that you discovered or realized about yourself while reading this book?
3. Why is it important for you to identify your True Potential and Self-Worth?
4. What can you do right now with what you have and where you are to make your life and those you care about full of Purpose?

PURPOSE NOTES

PURPOSE NOTES

P U R P O S E N O T E S

ABOUT DEMONT

    Demont Pope is a United States Air Force Veteran who grew up poor, while struggling to survive life in drug and crime infested neighborhoods. Growing up without his biological father, a victim of abuse, bullying, and attending 9 different schools, Demont suffered from rejection, depression, low self-esteem, insecurities, and low self worth. But that's not all. Yet, instead of allowing his circumstances to defeat him, Demont learned how to tap into his inner strength to become an authority on "The Power To Overcome".

For years he has been speaking to youth at group homes, detention centers, churches and schools. It's clear that Demont's true passion and purpose is to inspire and empower young minds. His mission is to add value to K-12 schools as well as colleges and universities by empowering and motivating at least 10 million students to realize their true Potential and Self Worth with his Motivational Speaking, Consulting, Books and Workshops.

Though Demont has many titles, his most valued are husband and father. The Pope family consists of his wife Niki and five kids; Amarien, Destiney, Demontez, Deanna, and little Demont. His bond with his own family is the driving force behind his passion for inspiring Youth and Young Adults. He chose to use his pain as power, his struggles as stepping stones, and his story as evidence of triumph and victory. For Demont, P.O.P.E. is more than just the spelling of his family name, it is a constant reminder to place "Purpose Over Pointless Excuses".

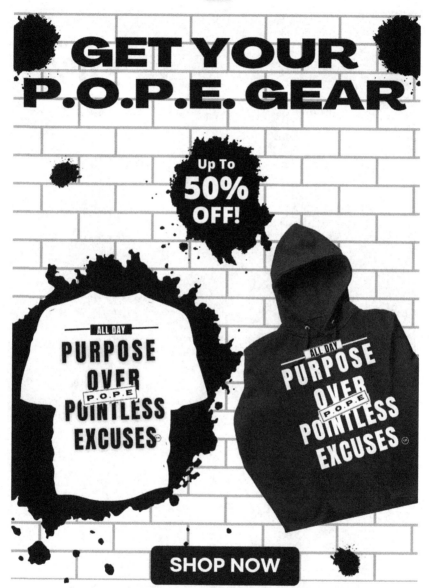

Purpose Over Pointless Excuses

Purpose Over Pointless Excuses

BOOK DEMONT

Demont is not just a Motivational Speaker, he is a Youth Advocate.

Topics Include:
Bullying
Good Decision Making
Leadership
Overcoming Adversity
Purpose
Respect
Self-Worth

Visit www.demontpope.com Today!

CONNECT WITH DEMONT

f   @ demontpope

◉   @ demontpope

in   @ demontpope

🐦   @ demontpope1

▶   @ demontpope

Purpose Over Pointless Excuses

PROFESSIONAL DEVELOPMENT

Presentation Topics:

Effective Communication
Motivation For Educators
Leadership
Relating to At-Risk Students
Self Care For Heroes

Visit: www.demontpope.com Today!

ORDER FOR YOUR STUDENTS

ATTENTION:
SCHOOLS, COLLEGES/UNIVERSITIES, EVENT COORDINATORS, and ORGANIZATIONS!

Purpose Over Pointless Excuses books are available at quantity **discounts** with bulk purchases.

Visit: www.demontpope.com or www.demontpopepublishing.com Today!

FREE RESOURCES

Available on **Apple Podcasts, Google Podcasts, Spotify, YouTube, and more!**

Search: ***Demont Pope*** or ***KING SPEAKS*** Podcast Today!

PURPOSE NOTES

PURPOSE NOTES

Purpose Over Pointless Excuses

P U R P O S E N O T E S

PURPOSE NOTES

Purpose Over Pointless Excuses

P U R P O S E N O T E S

Made in the USA
Columbia, SC
08 March 2025